Let's Find Out

Around-the-Year Mini-Books

9 Different, Irresistible Books that are Perfect for Beginning Readers

SCHOLASTIC
PROFESSIONAL BOOKS

New York ❄ Toronto ❄ London ❄ Auckland ❄ Sydney
Mexico City ❄ New Delhi ❄ Hong Kong

Cover design by Becky James

ISBN: 0-590-51308-7

Contents

Introduction

Welcome to Let's Find Out Around-the-Year Mini-books—a terrific way to introduce children to different kinds of written language all year long. Each mini-book combines warm and engaging illustrations with clear and simple text that invite children into the reading process.

Assembling the Books

Pull out each book along the perforated line. Cut in half along the dotted line and then insert the bottom page into the top to make a book of 8 pages. Staple the pages along the spine. (If you want to make the book more durable, cut out oaktag front and back covers and staple these along the spine along with the pages.)

Using the Books

The following summary will help you decide when and how to introduce each selection to children:

The Wheels on the Bus

Start the year with an old favorite. Many children will already know the song, and they can teach it to those who don't. The mini-book lends itself easily to dramatization, as children will naturally want to make the sounds illustrated in the pictures. And the little dog who wants to ride on the bus adds a new twist that all children will love.

The More We Get Together

Celebrate the beginning of the year with a favorite song! The repetitive text matched with a familiar tune draws children in and offers immediate ownership of the language of this mini-book. And the illustrations depict familiar classroom scenes in which children can count the growing number of friends made by a little girl.

Friends at School

Celebrate an important theme to children—friendship. This mini-book centers on the language of action. Children will encounter descriptive vocabulary for everyday school activities and are invited to compare the pictured classroom to their own.

Alike and Different

In consistent phrases that point out things that many children have in common, as well as things they do not have, this mini-book encourages readers to compare pictures and text. Classroom scenes again help children relate what they see in the story to their own lives.

Giving Thanks

Greet the holiday season with a mini-book that celebrates thankfulness. Patterned language helps frame familiar images in the context of giving thanks.

Over the River

Through rebus pictures, a favorite holiday song becomes a fun reading experience. Children can predict words in the song using the rebus guidelines, neatly summarized at the end of the mini-book.

More Than One

The end of the year signals growth. Here is a wonderful mini-book accessible to emergent readers, yet rich in vocabulary development as well. The funny and strange names given to groups of familiar animals is rendered in striking pictures of birds, fish, bees, pigs, and turtles dancing about.

The Turnip

This predictable Russian folk tale, ideal for the spring season when seeds are being planted, will delight children with its lesson about the joys and value of teamwork. After the first reading, children can participate in the reading by chanting the predictable second line, "The turnip would not come up!" This is a perfect literacy companion to a unit on planting or on a class experience with making soup.

Wake Up, It's Spring

The charm of a simple poem truly comes alive in this mini-book that celebrates the coming of spring. Predicting who will hear the seasonal news next will keep children actively involved from the first to the last page.

The Wheels on the Bus

SCHOLASTIC **Illustrated by James Williamson**

Cut along dotted lines. Put the pages in order to make a book.

The money on the bus goes clink, clink, clink.

The wheels on the bus go round and round.

The wipers on the bus go swish, swish, swish.

The people on the bus go hush, hush, hush.

The horn on the bus goes beep, beep, beep.

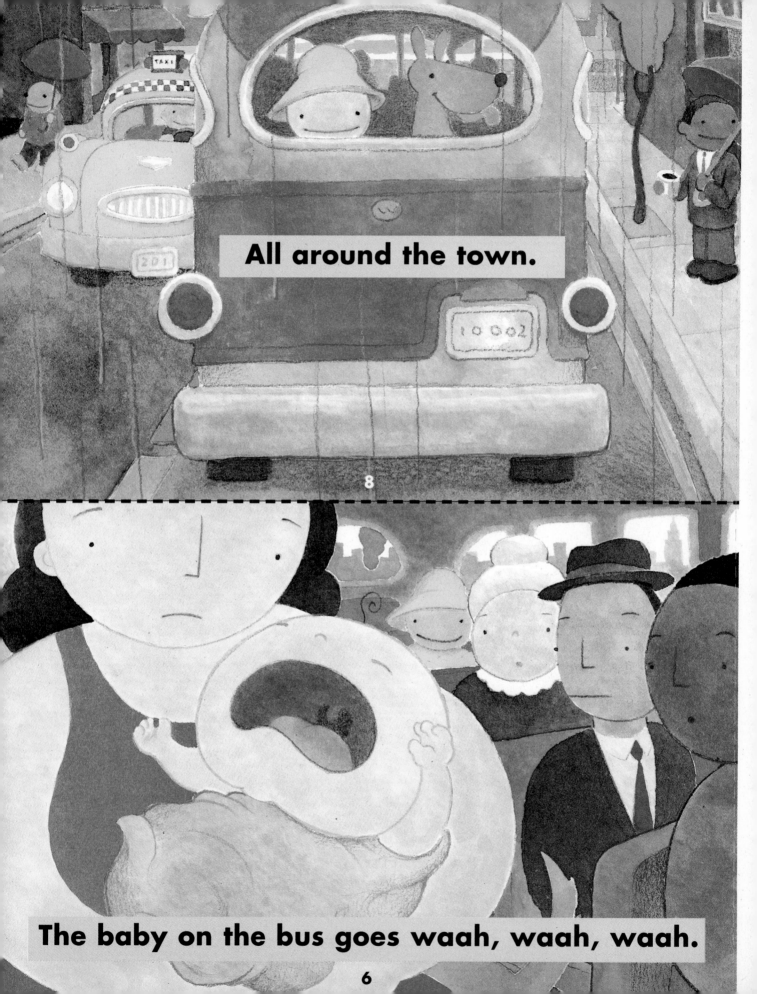

All around the town.

8

The baby on the bus goes waah, waah, waah.

6

The Wheels on the Bus

SCHOLASTIC

Illustrated by James Williamson

Cut along dotted lines. Put the pages in order to make a book.

The money on the bus goes clink, clink, clink.

The wheels on the bus go round and round.

The wipers on the bus go swish, swish, swish.

The people on the bus go hush, hush, hush.

The horn on the bus goes beep, beep, beep.

All around the town.

8

The baby on the bus goes waah, waah, waah.

6

The Wheels on the Bus

SCHOLASTIC   Illustrated by James Williamson

Cut along dotted lines. Put the pages in order to make a book.

The money on the bus goes clink, clink, clink.

3

The wheels on the bus go round and round.

STANTON ST.

DOWNTOWN

195

The wipers on the bus go swish, swish, swish.

The people on the bus go hush, hush, hush.

The horn on the bus goes beep, beep, beep.

All around the town.

8

The baby on the bus goes waah, waah, waah.

6

The Wheels on the Bus

SCHOLASTIC   **Illustrated by James Williamson**

Cut along dotted lines. Put the pages in order to make a book.

The money on the bus goes clink, clink, clink.

The wheels on the bus go round and round.

The wipers on the bus go swish, swish, swish.

The people on the bus go hush, hush, hush.

The horn on the bus goes beep, beep, beep.

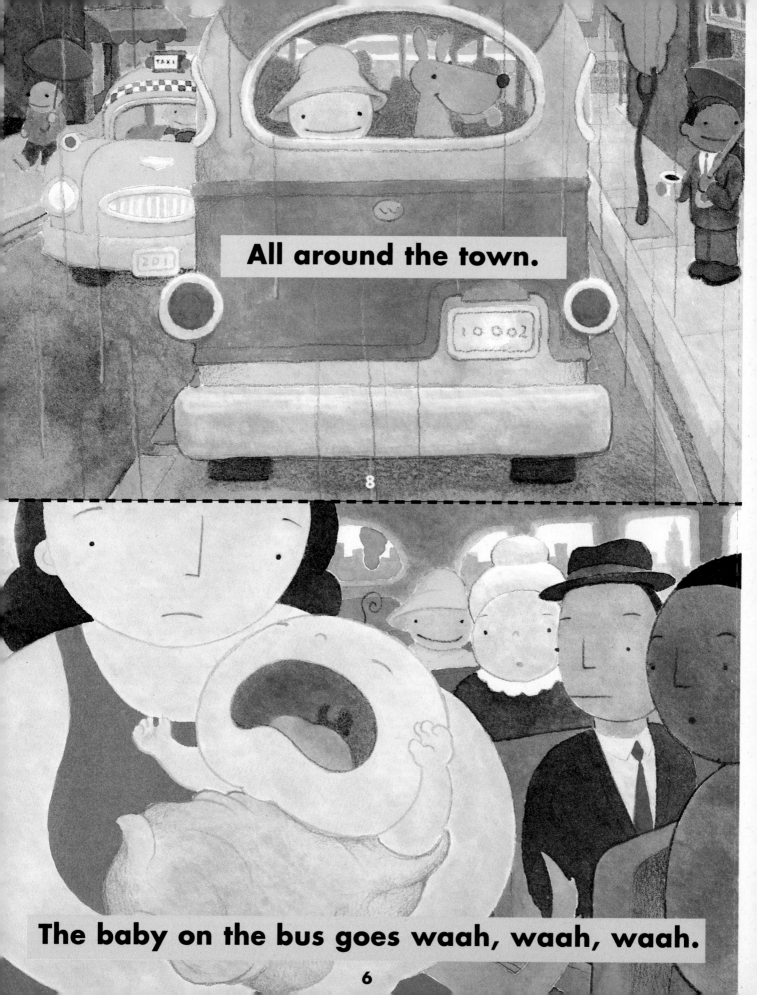

All around the town.

8

The baby on the bus goes waah, waah, waah.

6

The Wheels on the Bus

SCHOLASTIC   **Illustrated by James Williamson**

Cut along dotted lines. Put the pages in order to make a book.

The money on the bus goes clink, clink, clink.

The wheels on the bus go round and round.

The wipers on the bus go swish, swish, swish.

The people on the bus go hush, hush, hush.

The horn on the bus goes beep, beep, beep.

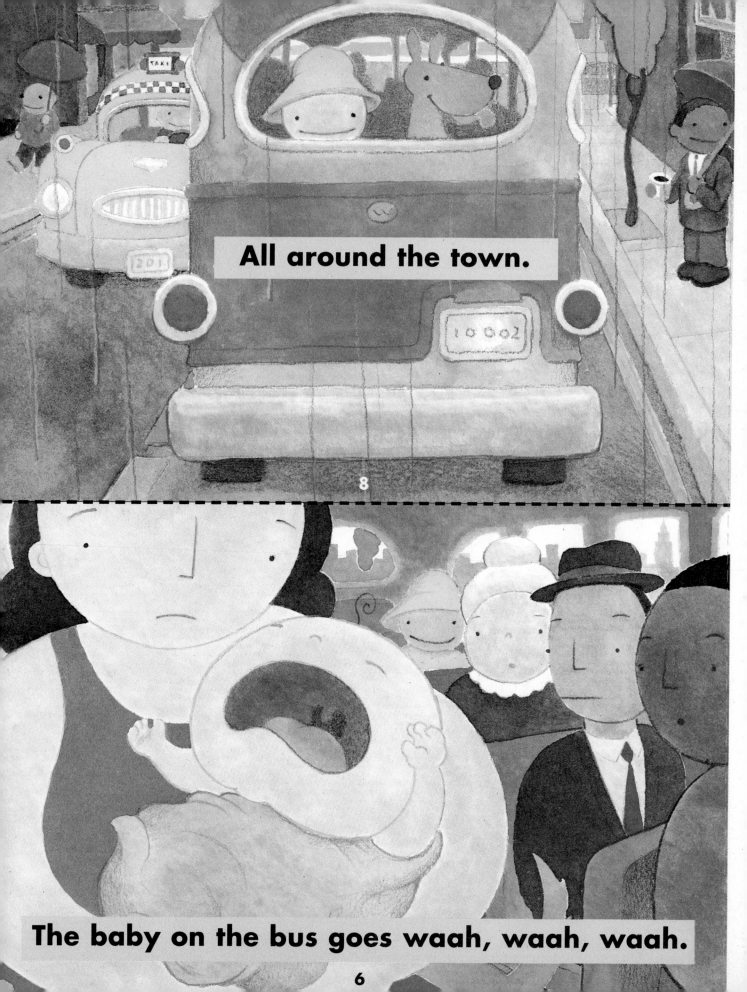

All around the town.

8

The baby on the bus goes waah, waah, waah.

6

The More We Get Together

SCHOLASTIC

1

- -

Cut along dotted lines. Put the pages in order to make a book.

Together, together,

3

The more we get together,

The more we get together,
The happier we'll be.

The more we get together,

For your friends are my friends,

The happier we'll be.

ILLUSTRATED BY BARI WEISSMAN

And my friends are your friends.

The More We Get Together

SCHOLASTIC

1

Cut along dotted lines. Put the pages in order to make a book.

Together, together,

3

The more we get together,

The more we get together,
The happier we'll be.

The more we get together,

7

For your friends are my friends,

5

The happier we'll be.

8

ILLUSTRATED BY BARI WEISSMAN

And my friends are your friends.

6

The More We Get Together

1

Cut along dotted lines. Put the pages in order to make a book.

Together, together,

3

The more we get together,

The more we get together,
The happier we'll be.

The more we get together,

For your friends are my friends,

The happier we'll be.

8

ILLUSTRATED BY BARI WEISSMAN

And my friends are your friends.

6

The More We Get Together

1

Cut along dotted lines. Put the pages in order to make a book.

Together, together,

3

The more we get together,

2

The more we get together,
The happier we'll be.

4

The more we get together,

For your friends are my friends,

The happier we'll be.

8

ILLUSTRATED BY BARI WEISSMAN

And my friends are your friends.

6

The More We Get Together

1

Cut along dotted lines. Put the pages in order to make a book.

Together, together,

3

The more we get together,

The more we get together,
The happier we'll be.

The more we get together,

For your friends are my friends,

The happier we'll be.

8

ILLUSTRATED BY BARI WEISSMAN

And my friends are your friends.

6

Friends at School

Hurrying, greeting, entering, meeting.

Cut along dotted lines. Put the pages in order to make a book.

Sharing, peeking, listening, speaking.

Gathering, giggling, sitting, wiggling.

2

Shoveling, thumping, scooping, dumping.

4

Petting, feeding, writing, reading.

Singing, humming, dancing, drumming.

Talking, showing, waving, going, GOOD-BYE!

8

Painting, drawing, hammering, sawing.

6

MINI-BOOK

LET'S FIND OUT

SEPTEMBER 1996

Friends at School

Hurrying, greeting, entering, meeting.

Cut along dotted lines. Put the pages in order to make a book.

Sharing, peeking, listening, speaking.

3

Gathering, giggling, sitting, wiggling.

2

Shoveling, thumping, scooping, dumping.

4

Petting, feeding, writing, reading.

7

Singing, humming, dancing, drumming.

5

Talking, showing, waving, going, GOOD-BYE!

8

Painting, drawing, hammering, sawing.

6

MINI-BOOK

LET'S FIND OUT

SEPTEMBER 1996

Friends at School

Hurrying, greeting, entering, meeting.

SCHOLASTIC

Cut along dotted lines. Put the pages in order to make a book.

Sharing, peeking, listening, speaking.

3

Gathering, giggling, sitting, wiggling.

2

Shoveling, thumping, scooping, dumping.

4

Petting, feeding, writing, reading.

Singing, humming, dancing, drumming.

Talking, showing, waving, going, GOOD-BYE!

Contains a minimum of 10% post-consumer fiber.

8

Painting, drawing, hammering, sawing.

6

Friends at School

Hurrying, greeting, entering, meeting.

■ SCHOLASTIC

Cut along dotted lines. Put the pages in order to make a book.

Sharing, peeking, listening, speaking.

Gathering, giggling, sitting, wiggling.

Shoveling, thumping, scooping, dumping.

Petting, feeding, writing, reading.

Singing, humming, dancing, drumming.

Talking, showing, waving, going, GOOD-BYE!

Painting, drawing, hammering, sawing.

Friends at School

Hurrying, greeting, entering, meeting.

SCHOLASTIC

Cut along dotted lines. Put the pages in order to make a book.

Sharing, peeking, listening, speaking.

3

Gathering, giggling, sitting, wiggling.

Shoveling, thumping, scooping, dumping.

Petting, feeding, writing, reading.

Singing, humming, dancing, drumming.

Talking, showing, waving, going, GOOD-BYE!

8

Painting, drawing, hammering, sawing.

6

LET'S FIND OUT

Alike and Different

Some of us have straight hair.

SCHOLASTIC

1

Cut along dotted lines. Put the pages in order to make a book.

Some of us have pigtails!

But we all have hair.

3

Some of us have curly hair.

Some of us have brown eyes.
Some of us have blue eyes.
Some of us wear glasses!

But we all have eyes.

Some of us like pizza.
Some of us like ice cream.
Some of us like broccoli!

But we all like to eat!

Some of us have darker skin.
Some of us have lighter skin.
Some of us have freckles!

But we all have skin.

Some of us like to pretend.
Some of us like to climb.
Some of us like to play ball.

BUT WE ALL like to play !

ILLUSTRATED BY LAURA CORNELL

Some of us wear sandals.
Some of us wear sneakers.
Some of us wear loafers.

But we all wear shoes.

LET'S FIND OUT

SEPTEMBER 1995

Alike and Different

Some of us have straight hair.

1

- -

Cut along dotted lines. Put the pages in order to make a book.

Some of us have pigtails!   But we all have hair.

3

Some of us have curly hair.

Some of us have brown eyes.
Some of us have blue eyes.
Some of us wear glasses!

But we all have eyes.

Some of us like pizza.
Some of us like ice cream.
Some of us like broccoli!

But we all like to eat!

7

Some of us have darker skin.
Some of us have lighter skin.
Some of us have freckles!

But we all have skin.

5

Some of us like to pretend.
Some of us like to climb.
Some of us like to play ball.

BUT WE ALL like to play !

8

ILLUSTRATED BY LAURA CORNELL

Some of us wear sandals.
Some of us wear sneakers.
Some of us wear loafers.

But we all wear shoes.

Alike and Different

Some of us have straight hair.

1

Cut along dotted lines. Put the pages in order to make a book.

Some of us have pigtails!   But we all have hair.

3

Some of us have curly hair.

Some of us have brown eyes.
Some of us have blue eyes.
Some of us wear glasses!

But we all have eyes.

Some of us like pizza.
Some of us like ice cream.
Some of us like broccoli!

But we all like to eat!

7

Some of us have darker skin.
Some of us have lighter skin.
Some of us have freckles!

But we all have skin.

5

Some of us like to pretend.
Some of us like to climb.
Some of us like to play ball.

BUT WE ALL like to play !

8

ILLUSTRATED BY LAURA CORNELL

Some of us wear sandals.
Some of us wear sneakers.
Some of us wear loafers.

But we all wear shoes.

LET'S FIND OUT

SEPTEMBER 1995

Alike and Different

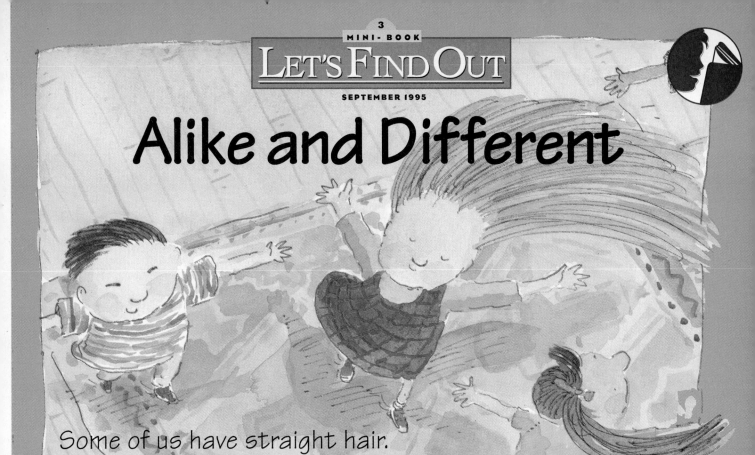

Some of us have straight hair.

SCHOLASTIC

1

Cut along dotted lines. Put the pages in order to make a book.

Some of us have pigtails!   But we all have hair.

3

Some of us have curly hair.

Some of us have brown eyes.
Some of us have blue eyes.
Some of us wear glasses!   But we all have eyes.

Some of us like pizza.
Some of us like ice cream.
Some of us like broccoli!

But we all like to eat!

Some of us have darker skin.
Some of us have lighter skin.
Some of us have freckles!

But we all have skin.

Some of us like to pretend.
Some of us like to climb.
Some of us like to play ball.

BUT WE ALL like to play !

8

ILLUSTRATED BY LAURA CORNELL

Some of us wear sandals.
Some of us wear sneakers.
Some of us wear loafers.

But we all wear shoes.

6

LET'S FIND OUT

SEPTEMBER 1995

Alike and Different

Some of us have straight hair.

1

Cut along dotted lines. Put the pages in order to make a book.

Some of us have pigtails!   But we all have hair.

3

Some of us have curly hair.

Some of us have brown eyes.
Some of us have blue eyes.
Some of us wear glasses!

But we all have eyes.

Some of us like pizza.
Some of us like ice cream.
Some of us like broccoli!

But we all like to eat!

Some of us have darker skin.
Some of us have lighter skin.
Some of us have freckles!

But we all have skin.

Some of us like to pretend.
Some of us like to climb.
Some of us like to play ball.

BUT WE ALL like to play !

8

ILLUSTRATED BY LAURA CORNELL

Some of us wear sandals.
Some of us wear sneakers.
Some of us wear loafers.

But we all wear shoes.

Giving Thanks

Thanks for fathers.
Thanks for mothers,
Thanks for little, tiny baby brothers!

1

Cut along dotted lines. Put the pages in order to make a book.

Thanks for crunchy leaves and little bugs!

3

Thanks for kisses.
Thanks for hugs.

Thanks for secrets.
Thanks for chats.

Thanks for families...

Thanks for puppies, dogs, kittens, and cats!

Getting together!

ILLUSTRATED BY JAMES HALE

Thanks for stars.
Thanks for weather.

Giving Thanks

Thanks for fathers.
Thanks for mothers,
Thanks for little, tiny baby brothers!

SCHOLASTIC

1

Cut along dotted lines. Put the pages in order to make a book.

Thanks for crunchy leaves and little bugs!

3

Thanks for kisses.
Thanks for hugs.

Thanks for secrets.
Thanks for chats.

Thanks for families...

Thanks for puppies, dogs, kittens, and cats!

Getting together!

ILLUSTRATED BY JAMES HALE

Thanks for stars.
Thanks for weather.

Giving Thanks

Thanks for fathers.
Thanks for mothers,
Thanks for little, tiny baby brothers!

1

Cut along dotted lines. Put the pages in order to make a book.

Thanks for crunchy leaves and little bugs!

3

Thanks for kisses.
Thanks for hugs.

2

Thanks for secrets.
Thanks for chats.

4

Thanks for families...

Thanks for puppies, dogs, kittens, and cats!

Getting together!

ILLUSTRATED BY JAMES HALE

Thanks for stars.
Thanks for weather.

LET'S FIND OUT

NOV/DEC 1995

Giving Thanks

Thanks for fathers.
Thanks for mothers.
Thanks for little, tiny baby brothers!

1

Cut along dotted lines. Put the pages in order to make a book.

Thanks for crunchy leaves and little bugs!

3

Thanks for kisses.
Thanks for hugs.

2

Thanks for secrets.
Thanks for chats.

4

Thanks for families...

Thanks for puppies, dogs, kittens, and cats!

Getting together!

8

ILLUSTRATED BY JAMES HALE

Thanks for stars.
Thanks for weather.

6

Giving Thanks

Thanks for fathers.
Thanks for mothers,
Thanks for little, tiny baby brothers!

1

Cut along dotted lines. Put the pages in order to make a book.

Thanks for crunchy leaves and little bugs!

3

Thanks for kisses.
Thanks for hugs.

Thanks for secrets.
Thanks for chats.

Thanks for families...

Thanks for puppies, dogs, kittens, and cats!

Getting together!

8

ILLUSTRATED BY JAMES HALE

Thanks for stars.
Thanks for weather.

6

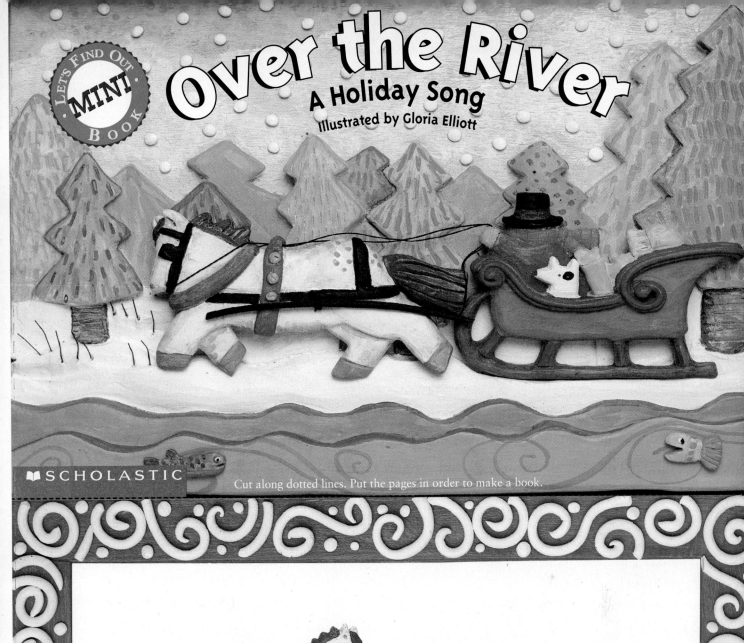

Cut along dotted lines. Put the pages in order to make a book.

The  knows the way

To carry the

3

Over the

And through the

To Grandmother's we go.

2

Through the white and drifted .

4

It stings the

And bites the

As over the we go.

7

Over the

And through the

5

river

snow

woods

wind

house

nose

horse

toes

sleigh

ground

Oh, how the does blow!

6

Over the River
A Holiday Song
Illustrated by Gloria Elliott

LET'S FIND OUT MINI BOOK

SCHOLASTIC

Cut along dotted lines. Put the pages in order to make a book.

The  knows the way

To carry the

3

Over the

And through the

To Grandmother's we go.

2

Through the white and drifted .

4

It stings the

And bites the

As over the we go.

7

Over the

And through the

5

river

snow

woods

wind

house

nose

horse

toes

sleigh

ground

Oh, how the ___ does blow!

Over the River
A Holiday Song
Illustrated by Gloria Elliott

SCHOLASTIC

Cut along dotted lines. Put the pages in order to make a book.

The  knows the way

To carry the

3

Over the

And through the

To Grandmother's we go.

2

Through the white and drifted .

4

It stings the

And bites the

As over the we go.

7

Over the

And through the

5

river

snow

woods

wind

house

nose

horse

toes

sleigh

ground

Oh, how the does blow!

6

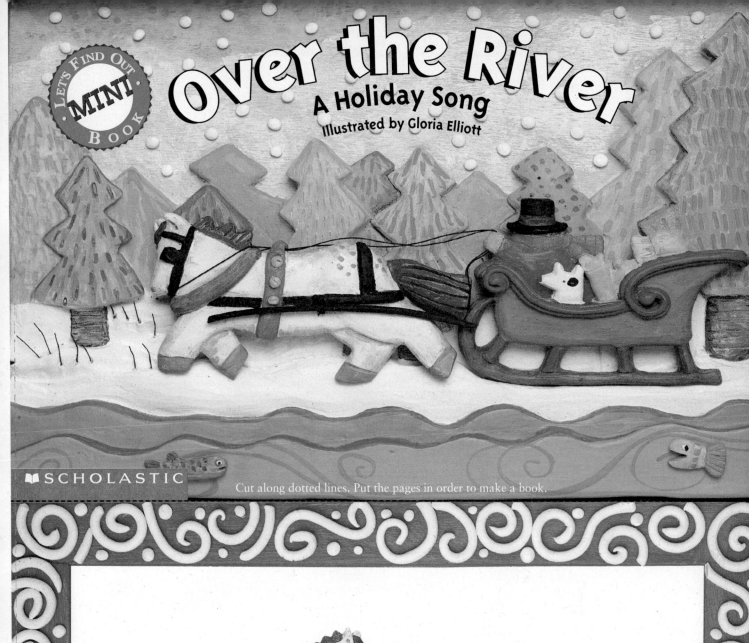

Over the River
A Holiday Song
Illustrated by Gloria Elliott

LETS FIND OUT MINI BOOK

SCHOLASTIC

Cut along dotted lines. Put the pages in order to make a book.

The  knows the way

To carry the

3

Over the

And through the

To Grandmother's we go.

2

Through the white and drifted .

4

It stings the

And bites the

As over the we go.

7

Over the

And through the

5

	river		snow
house	woods		wind
	house		nose
	horse		toes
	sleigh		ground

Oh, how the does blow!

6

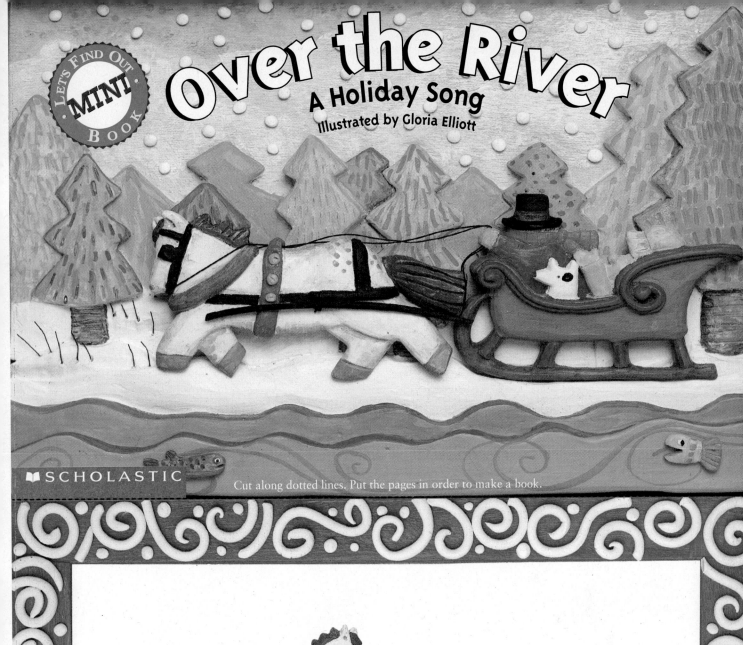

Over the River
A Holiday Song
Illustrated by Gloria Elliott

Cut along dotted lines. Put the pages in order to make a book.

SCHOLASTIC

The  knows the way

To carry the

3

Over the

And through the

To Grandmother's we go.

2

Through the white and drifted .

4

It stings the

And bites the

As over the we go.

7

Over the

And through the

5

 river	snow			

river

woods

house

horse

sleigh

snow

wind

nose

toes

ground

Oh, how the does blow!

More Than One

Illustrated by Daniel Moreton

SCHOLASTIC

Cut along dotted lines. Put the pages in order to make a book.

A flock of birds.

One bird...

One fish...

4

A swarm of bees.

7

A school of fish.

5

More Than One

A bale   **A litter**

One bee...

More Than One

Illustrated by Daniel Moreton

■SCHOLASTIC

Cut along dotted lines. Put the pages in order to make a book.

A flock of birds.

3

One bird...

2

One fish...

4

A swarm of bees.

7

A school of fish.

5

More Than One

A bale

A litter

8

One bee...

6

LET'S FIND OUT
· MINI ·
BOOK

Illustrated by Daniel Moreton

■SCHOLASTIC

Cut along dotted lines. Put the pages in order to make a book.

A flock of birds.

One bird...

2

One fish...

4

A **swarm** of bees.

A **school** of fish.

More Than One

A bale

A litter

One bee...

More Than One

Illustrated by Daniel Moreton

SCHOLASTIC

Cut along dotted lines. Put the pages in order to make a book.

A flock of birds.

3

One bird...

One fish...

A swarm of bees.

7

A school of fish.

5

More Than One

A bale

A litter

One bee...

LET'S FIND OUT
MINI
BOOK

More Than One

Illustrated by Daniel Moreton

SCHOLASTIC

Cut along dotted lines. Put the pages in order to make a book.

A flock of birds.

3

One bird...

One fish...

4

A **swarm** of bees.

A **school** of fish.

More Than One

A bale

A litter

One bee...

LET'S FIND OUT

OCTOBER 1995

The Turnip
A Russian Folktale

Grandpa planted a turnip.
It grew very big.
He could not pull it out of the ground.

1

Cut along dotted lines. Put the pages in order to make a book.

Eva came to help.
The turnip would not come up!

3

Grandma came to help.
The turnip would not come up!

2

Dog came to help.
The turnip would not come up!

4

Mouse helped anyway!

Cat came to help.
The turnip would not come up!

The turnip came out of the ground!
"Now we can all have soup!" said Mouse.

JOHANNE WEILBRENNER

8

Mouse came to help.
"You're too small to help!" they all said.

6

LET'S FIND OUT

OCTOBER 1995

The Turnip
A Russian Folktale

Grandpa planted a turnip.
It grew very big.
He could not pull it out of the ground.

SCHOLASTIC

1

Cut along dotted lines. Put the pages in order to make a book.

Eva came to help.
The turnip would not come up!

3

Grandma came to help.
The turnip would not come up!

2

Dog came to help.
The turnip would not come up!

4

Mouse helped anyway!

Cat came to help.
The turnip would not come up!

The turnip came out of the ground!
"Now we can all have soup!" said Mouse.

JOHANNE WEILBRENNER

Mouse came to help.
"You're too small to help!" they all said.

LET'S FIND OUT

OCTOBER 1995

The Turnip
A Russian Folktale

Grandpa planted a turnip.
It grew very big.
He could not pull it out of the ground.

1

Cut along dotted lines. Put the pages in order to make a book.

Eva came to help.
The turnip would not come up!

3

Grandma came to help.
The turnip would not come up!

2

Dog came to help.
The turnip would not come up!

4

Mouse helped anyway!

Cat came to help.
The turnip would not come up!

The turnip came out of the ground!
"Now we can all have soup!" said Mouse.

8

JOHANNE WEILBRENNER

Mouse came to help.
"You're too small to help!" they all said.

LET'S FIND OUT
OCTOBER 1995

The Turnip
A Russian Folktale

Grandpa planted a turnip.
It grew very big.
He could not pull it out of the ground.

1

Cut along dotted lines. Put the pages in order to make a book.

Eva came to help.
The turnip would not come up!

3

Grandma came to help.
The turnip would not come up!

2

Dog came to help.
The turnip would not come up!

4

Mouse helped anyway!

Cat came to help.
The turnip would not come up!

The turnip came out of the ground!
"Now we can all have soup!" said Mouse.

8

JOHANNE WEILBRENNER

Mouse came to help.
"You're too small to help!" they all said.

6

LET'S FIND OUT

OCTOBER 1995

The Turnip
A Russian Folktale

Grandpa planted a turnip.
It grew very big.
He could not pull it out of the ground.

1

Cut along dotted lines. Put the pages in order to make a book.

Eva came to help.
The turnip would not come up!

3

Grandma came to help.
The turnip would not come up!

2

Dog came to help.
The turnip would not come up!

4

Mouse helped anyway!

Cat came to help.
The turnip would not come up!

The turnip came out of the ground!
"Now we can all have soup!" said Mouse.

8

JOHANNE WEILBRENNER

Mouse came to help.
"You're too small to help!" they all said.

Wake Up, It's Spring!

by Pamela Chanko & Samantha Berger

illustrated by Kevin O'Malley

LET'S FIND OUT · MINI · BOOK

SCHOLASTIC

Cut along dotted lines. Put the pages in order to make a book.

The rabbit hopped and thumped his feet
To tell the deer the air smelled sweet.

3

In April the robin began to sing
To tell the rabbit it was spring.

2

The little deer ran with the bunny
To tell the duck the sky was sunny.

4

The mouse just made a tiny peep
To tell the birds to start to cheep.

7

The duck swam off and gave a quack
To tell the cows "The leaves are back!"

5

Then all the birds began to sing
To tell the bear "Wake up, it's spring!"

8

The cow let out a long, low moo
To tell the mouse that flowers grew.

6

Wake Up, It's Spring!

by Pamela Chanko & Samantha Berger

illustrated by Kevin O'Malley

Cut along dotted lines. Put the pages in order to make a book.

The rabbit hopped and thumped his feet
To tell the deer the air smelled sweet.

In April the robin began to sing
To tell the rabbit it was spring.

2

The little deer ran with the bunny
To tell the duck the sky was sunny.

4

The mouse just made a tiny peep
To tell the birds to start to cheep.

7

The duck swam off and gave a quack
To tell the cows "The leaves are back!"

5

Then all the birds began to sing
To tell the bear "Wake up, it's spring!"

8

The cow let out a long, low moo
To tell the mouse that flowers grew.

6

Wake Up, It's Spring!

by Pamela Chanko & Samantha Berger

illustrated by Kevin O'Malley

Cut along dotted lines. Put the pages in order to make a book.

The rabbit hopped and thumped his feet
To tell the deer the air smelled sweet.

3

In April the robin began to sing
To tell the rabbit it was spring.

2

The little deer ran with the bunny
To tell the duck the sky was sunny.

4